Be About It Press

# Blueberry Lemonade

## Marzi Margo

**2nd Edition**

**Be About It Press**
**January 2021**

**cover design by Carmen E. Brady**

ISBN: 978-0-9986012-6-7

4

This book was originally published by Bottlecap Press in 2015. Some of these poems first appeared in the following publications:

*Anime Dad Review, Bottlec[r]ap, Bravehost Poetry Review, Dead Snakes, Electric Cereal, Guide to Kulchur Creative Journal, Haiku Journal, Heavy Contortionists, Hip Hop Hooray Press, Hipster Jesus Unicorn, Internet Poetry, Metazen, New Wave Vomit, Poetry by Emily Dickinson, Sadcore Dadwave, Screaming Seahorse, Sprout Zine, Sunlit,* & *Welter.*

This second edition is dedicated to
Kristie, Molly, Addy, Peter, Melissa, Angel, & Dad.

# table of contents

my existential plights entail nothing in
comparison to the struggles of
chicago's homeless

you glue a broken dreamcatcher together
& think that it is you

you hang a black velvet painting of red skelton on the
    wall
& think that it is you

you eat a bowl of stale apple jacks
& think that it is you

you read a poem by blueberry morningsnow before
    you drive to work
& think that it is you

you watch a drop of bird shit splatter onto your
    windshield
& think that it is you

you order a small vanilla milkshake from a fast food
    restaurant
& think that it is you

you pull the trigger on a plastic toy gun that you have
    put into your mouth
& think that it is you

you find a quarter underneath your bed
& think that it is you


you have a terrifying nightmare in which you are
    being attacked by zombies who do not look like
    reanimated corpses but just ordinary living people
    with ordinary lives & you try to pray to god that
    the zombies will not claw your eyes out with their
    warm fingers or start a conversation with you
    about the newest presidential candidate &
    whether or not they would ever vote for them but
    then you realize that there is no god in this horrid
    dream world & then the zombies' hands & voices
    reach you & you are dying & you have never felt
    more afraid because all of the zombies look
    exactly like the people you will see tomorrow on
    the street & at the office & in your apartment &
    again & again & again & you sweat your way
    through this nightmare
& think that it is you

## washington, lincoln, lafayette

it is the beginning of the summer
& everywhere feels too hot
the ice cream truck circles its usual route
with a lonesome echo
its jingle keeps asking
"hello?"
as if to beg for the attention of this tired city
the kids are tired & the kids' hands are exhausted
the sno-cones are desperate to melt
melting over sweaty fingers
or melting over thirsty tongues
mixing with either saliva or cement
bare toes burning on black roads
my next-door neighbors turn on the radio
& fill up the inflatable pool
the ice cream truck drives around until it no longer
    exists
& then all of us look right through the sky
waiting for nightfall

## blueberry

i am sick of reading poems about the ocean
i am sick of reading poems about birds or clouds
i initiated the attack & my mind was blown
i came into the world fucking
i will go up in smoke
i am alive!
when i am falling asleep, i can transform any room
so lonely, i have urges
so lonely, i have needs
fuck science
fuck research
fuck disease
i'm channeling my feelings into art tonight
i'm not cut out for academia
i'm cut out for sleeping
i'm not a man
i am dirt in everything, i am dirt
i am listening to ashlee simpson
i want to know everything about captain america
toy stores suddenly appeal to me again
don't we see the bones we walk on?
we weave sandals & leave them secretly by the
    roadside
we have different opinions
in the end though, i just want people to participate
in any way possible

# bombshell vocations

at the nightclub dances
the prettiest matter
across a summit of storms

a modish windmill at the diehard café
taming waves & riding tight corners
in an underground room
on a wordless night still transient

like ghost hands over heavens
hammering out an age
of permanence or fence
sustained in isolation

let me push this trial & at once
kowtow to these arabian cascades
& sidewalk muses
for their large-scale wisdom
told after the heavy rains

against a backdrop
the monuments glisten
with light spring rain

the hands rise over a snowstorm
loftily living & blooming
safe from harm in a simplified city
rasping into a saw-like slip
of vintage wear & leisure time

cloaked in ameliorated cleanliness
they echo oral accounts of love said aloud
forbidding any unexpected fish farm frost

yapping about quick friendship
& the slow dark moon
vultures speak in heated murmurs
their lowly souls with salty patches
into slow synthetic synthesis

the old adage is nothing more
than a true hope shudder
bluish flags treading water

bliss is not fixed in passing canisters
of gin or the sap of the sin
that came to humanity
in punctured lines

chiming of different times
at a monday morning's rally
the comedians & magicians
come together in search of footprints

as they move on
they recite their own songs
clacking & passing jars
to make ready
for the revolution of thorns

## eight or nine short stories that i really enjoy

"remember, relive" by deborah willis
"fuck coolhunter" by ysabel sex
"the open window" by saki
"saved by the bell" by sam pink
"cain rose up" by stephen king
"an encounter" by james joyce
"swimming in the house of the sea" by jeremy robert
    johnson
"a real doll" by a.m. homes
"in the cemetery where al jolson is buried" by amy
    hempel

## ten titles of poems that i will never write

i hate being alone, but i also hate bothering other
people

trying

after my death, everyone i ever knew will come
together to build a statue in my honor, then
promptly demolish it & celebrate the ruins

manor #55,208

possession (amplified)

an emotional spectrum as represented by assorted
shades of pink

at a river, determining whether to drink from it or
drown in it

the sun is nothing more than an apparition's eyeball

pipe dream of being reincarnated as a copy of the nes
game "pipe dream"

bare hug

# thirteen haiku

## haiku for disappointment

i cannot sing well
enough for you to like me
enough to love me

-

## haiku for disillusionment

i want to live a
life that consists of drinking,
writing, & loving

-

## haiku for doubt

what is persistence
but to refuse to give up
& to keep failing?

## haiku for entropy

remove me from here
peel my skin like crops & keep
my bones in a bag

-

## haiku for guilt

i am so sorry
please forgive me. i am a
monster. i hate it

-

## haiku for healing

two dayquil capsules
i will swallow these & then
i will feel better

-

## haiku for hope

i dream of being
a skyscraper in the midst
of a hurricane

18

## haiku for insomnia

at midnight, i think
about the happiness we'll
share only in thoughts

-

## haiku for loneliness

call me. please. i miss
you & need validation
that you miss me too

-

## haiku for pestilence

i will fall more ill
than the sickest children. you
are like a virus

-

## haiku for sublimity

the sky splits open
& a waterfall rushes
from the void like light

## haiku for us

you & i are on
a spaceship together &
we are both happy

-

## haiku for you

i am listening
to ragtime jazz & wishing
you were here with me

## tanka for my unhappy friends

i would spend my whole
life unhappy if it meant
that all of my friends
who struggle so much each day
could live the happiest lives

## the glorious inexplicability of feeling some type of way

watching videos of spiders wrapping wasps in their
    webs
evokes an active desire to become passively
    enveloped

the song "lifestyle" by rich gang feat. young thug &
    rich homie quan
liquefies itself & replaces all of my internal fluids

between zaytoven beats, i hear crickets competing
    against police sirens
& i feel so content with the entropy of the universe

a spider & a rapper seem to bear the same intention
carving beauty out of rhythm & what's been inherited
    from history

i suddenly fall in love with everything whether it will
    slay me or not
i decide that someday i will offer you the blue of the
    moon

## a fun activity for a sunday afternoon:

lie on the floor & stare at the wall & think about all of
the people you are in love with who will never be
in love with you

think about the human body & all of its pieces

sometimes the heart feels like an apple & sometimes
it feels like an apple core

sometimes there is nothing else to do but wait

whenever i'm waiting, i don't understand what i'm
waiting for

& whenever i'm feeling like i want to be in a romantic
relationship with someone, i don't understand
what it even means to be in a romantic
relationship with someone

my heart feels heavy inside of my body like a glass
paperweight

& trying to divert my attention away from my own
mortality & meaninglessness by focusing on my
breathing only causes my arms to tremble

## i left my house today

i walked down the middle of the street
there were no cars in sight
i couldn't hear anything around me
no wind whistling
no birds chirping
no children shouting
no lawnmowers rumbling
just the sound of my nervous system in operation
& the sound of my blood in circulation
nothing else even seemed to exist
i left my house today hoping to grow
but instead only realized
that i would always be somehow
housed inside of myself

## twofold

at that exact moment
i knew what the future would deliver
on the final night of my first summer
& added shades of white to the air
i stood with the blue paint at my disposal
as a lonesome human being
& i felt capable of embracing it all
miles & miles beyond
i was an artist at last
i climbed the rooftops of my city
i scrambled to the peak of every skyscraper
the artist that i had always strived to be

## do-it-yourself make-a-wish foundation

to whom it may not concern:
it concerns me
& that is that
if your hand is as big as your face
it means that you have cancer
& if you ask me to marry you
then the answer is yes
yes i am an ugly human being
yes i do have a heart

## snow monster

december
at night
i feel as if the waiting
will never end

this windowsill
is too cold
i don't see how
things will ever be okay
after what's happening
outside

can we meet somewhere
in my bed?
drive over & park
on the street
knock twice
i'll be upstairs
the door should be
unlocked
it always is

meet me in my bedroom
join me in this bed
write love songs with me
on this college-ruled
notebook paper
i promise that i won't
cross out
any of your lyrics

my bedspread is electric
we can be warmer
than god will permit us
please sleep
i've never been this tired

## bodies of 60% water

the flood is falling
daintily
down

down from my ancestors
down the field

my brainwaves
on vacation
flood

& envision your expression
in the moon's visage

the social soul that
beyond me
flooded

no less than
whatever i am

you get the drift
the flora
the fauna

i
you

at no time stand
common
cold

as the flood
unfolds

your figure so
infinitesimal
insubstantial

& in time untold
i do not hanker after her

given that i am put to sleep
by your honey spell
your speak'n'smell

the party in the parallel
no forced feeling

no belief ne'er blubbered
makes me consider
the layers over

the muscles of the mental
define our aura

she they
you sway
stagger

& shake the walls
when floods attack

plain & fruited
my majesty
purple

mountain's peak
branches

& i
let you
move me

by whatever method
you regard a remark

length
&
breadth

## dragon daisies

i am naked & feeling like the spectre of death
& these walls died in 1994

my first encounter with an earthquake shakes virginia
& new york melting in the snow
how soon they forget

but seriously
woof woof woof woof woof

i struggle to shave
with all my chest hair
exposed

my jawline is bleeding
the left side of my neck hurts

my face is so angular
i am socially awkward
i am very tired

i am going to lie down
until there is something good on tv

i hate tv
i have a big date next thursday
gore me

## untitled

a live video feed of me sitting in front of my computer
silently reading a book of poetry by alexandra
    naughton
listening to trap rap beats
it's too hot in my bedroom
too hot in my house
my neighborhood
my city
my state
my country
myspace
facebook
there is only the internet
my digital identity is all that exists
this live video feed is all that exists
offer me free access to gucci mane's complete
    discography
teach me about optimism & the art of zen
choose your words carefully
& understand just how desperately i need them

## a garbage bag stuffed with internal organs

when i am woken up by the afternoon sunlight
  beaming through my window

sometimes i find myself lying in my bed in the same
  position that a corpse lies in its casket

& i think that this happens because sometimes i
  dream of dying

& it just feels so right

# blessa

still a turn-of-the-century child
fifteen years into the twenty-first century

with a bag of pills in my pocket
& a lottery ticket left at home somewhere

i hock loogies over bridges & i vote
i lost my hands in the great human war

to all the people who dialed
nine-one-one on nine-eleven

& wept for the skylines
at breakfast the next day

you are here & you are clean
& i want you to come wander with me

away from this place of purple
mountains & shattered glass

to a land of virgin sacrifices
& all-you-can-eat shrimp

## you live on a farm somewhere in the midwest

the farm belongs to your father
or maybe your grandfather
i can't remember

on the night that we met
you told me about your first experience with death

you were a little girl & you'd given every cow a funny
    name
you thought that the cows were just your family's
    pets
& someone had to tell you the truth about the cows

then your father slaughtered your favorite cow
the one that had the funniest name

your family ate hamburgers for dinner that week
you cried for a long time but eventually recovered
& now you know not to get too attached to the cattle

when my friends & i picked you up from the farm,
    you looked so young & pretty
& when we dropped you off later that night, there
    was something older in your smile

## you were thunder

you were a woodscrew between two piano strings
you were the white ghost haunting an erased
    blackboard
you were the aftermath of your mouth swallowing
    mine
you were an abandoned factory aflame

you were a natural nightmare
you were the longest word ever printed on paper
you were the green beacon beyond the sea
you were an animal without a cage

you were a presence to be known
you were the red to poseidon's blue
you were the sentence left unuttered
you were an artist as much as an audience

you were a monument of slate
you were the answer to the prisoners' prayers
you were the favorite cousin at the dinner party
you were an invisibility cloak

you were a wonderful memory
you were the intersection
you were the plastic bag drifting down the street
you were an enigma

you were a promise never broken
you were the movie never made
you were the original blues musician
you were an entropy of cells

## whenever i hear this song

i recall the day that we met outside the concert venue
& the show was sold out
& i'd purchased my ticket in advance
& you hadn't
& we decided to forget about the opening bands
& go to a bar somewhere nearby
& we went to a bar somewhere nearby
& drank fruity cocktails until we both felt giggly
& carefree
& at one point you were excited to tell me something
& you threw your cheese quesadilla without thinking
& it bounced across the table
& we laughed so hard that our stomachs hurt
& eventually we realized that the headlining band had
    probably started playing
& we walked back to the concert venue
& we said goodbye outside the concert venue
& you started to walk back to the bus station
& then i discovered that they were selling extra
    tickets at the door
& then i chased after you to inform you of my
    discovery
& then you were able to purchase a ticket after all
& we were able to see the show together
& we danced next to each other for what seemed like
    hours
& we were still so drunk
& joyful

& at the end of the night you told me that healing
    comes from within
& i drove home while listening to this song
& feeling happier than i'd felt in such a long time

# lemonade

the entire room smells like sweat & lemons
the bedsheets are stained with yellow
gucci mane's "when i was water whippin" blares from
the stereo of a passing car
i yawn & you smile & say that i yawn like a cheetah

the bedsheets are stained with yellow
outside it is 98 degrees & our air conditioner is broken
i yawn & you smile & say that i yawn like a cheetah
you ask me where we should eat after steven's party
tonight & i say "i don't know"

outside it is 98 degrees & our air conditioner is broken
you say "we could eat at taco bell again" & i look at
you & grin
you ask me where we should eat after steven's party
tonight & i say "i don't know"
"so what do you want to do now?" you ask me

you say "we could eat at taco bell again" & i look at
you & grin
the broken air conditioner falls out of our window &
crashes to the floor
"so what do you want to do now?" you ask me
"let's wash these sheets" i say

## they told me i could be anything i wanted to be, so i killed myself

it is 1:37am & i've been drinking too much coffee
i feel my stomach ache like a night in november
every night feels the same way anymore
like a tub of glue being poured into a canyon

i feel my stomach ache like a night in november
when the stars burn blue outside my window
like a tub of glue being poured into a canyon
somewhere in tanzania, an elephant is dying

when the stars burn blue outside my window
i know that i should be in bed
somewhere in tanzania, an elephant is dying
& i've never felt more powerless

i know that i should be in bed
but the caffeine in my system won't let me sleep
& i've never felt more powerless
& the future has never seemed so uncertain

## devil's son-in-law

i am an abstract expressionist painting
i want to melt on your wall
i eat a six-month-old cherry-flavored tic-tac
it tastes like poison but i swallow it

i want to melt on your wall
i take a sip of warm mountain dew
it tastes like poison but i swallow it
& pour the rest of the can down the toilet

i take a sip of warm mountain dew
after eating an overcooked hot dog
& pour the rest of the can down the toilet
singing a song by peetie wheatstraw

after eating an overcooked hot dog
i lie down on the bathroom floor
singing a song by peetie wheatstraw
"don't feel welcome blues"

## the wanderer

i want to walk through you
like water passing through a nanny's hands
as she draws a bath for her boss's child
delicate & passive & so full of light

like water passing through a nanny's hands
just as a grain of sand is lifted by the wind
delicate & passive & so full of light
my ghosts await a home to haunt

just as a grain of sand is lifted by the wind
i have become a passenger of my own momentum
my ghosts await a home to haunt
a destination worth drifting towards

i have become a passenger of my own momentum
hoping but never trying to find
a destination worth drifting towards
& a stranger worth meeting there

# &&&&&&&

every home is a haunted house & every mirror is a
    zoo
the mirror in the mirror like my face behind my face
the death march to my dorm after yet another class
it all glows with a certain shade of orange
i feel like such a stupid bastard
& i want to drown in concrete

i listen to musique concrète
feeling like an animal in a zoo
a new breed of pathetic bastard
with some fresh & hideous face
outside the sky has turned orange
& i don't want to go back to class

the realization that i have fallen asleep in class
is the same as the realization that nothing is concrete
that my experience of peeling & then eating an
    orange
is as abstract as the idea of the universe being one
    dark, infinite zoo
just a single idea out of the many that i will never
    actually have to face
& yet that idea continues to terrorize me as if it were
    an unwanted bastard

i myself am an unmannered bastard
rude & repulsive, no conception of class
i try to distract myself by thinking about your face
when you swing your sledgehammer & smash my
    skull all over the concrete
then scrape up the specks of brain matter to put on
    display in your personal zoo
& when all the red goo on the sidewalk is hardened
    by the sun, it turns a murky orange

my entire existence hardens & turns a murky orange
as i dance alone to the greatest hits of ol' dirty
    bastard
"cold blooded," "shimmy shimmy ya," "brooklyn zoo"
after a while, i decide that i'm never going back to
    class
after a while, i explode & an orange goo covers the
    walls of concrete
& the goo hardens & the walls crumble & all that is
    left is your laughing face

there isn't a face that i would like to kiss more than
    your face
your kiss tastes like kiwi, maybe with a hint of orange
but nothing is permanent because nothing is concrete
mordred was a bastard & i too am a bastard
a steelyard kid, middle class
& keeper of the zoo

my own orange zoo
my own concrete face
& my own bastard class

## tarantula

its strength
crinkled by wealth

useful for the psyche
convulsion begins

dreams immense, hopes losing
yet to be

what you accomplish
unshakable devotion in our sights

a noise today
out there but not unaided

left to say to you at times
singe all passages

shallow call in the dark
take a trail

survive the study
facts reaching a decision

a kingdom similar to this
friendship in reality

fresh loop
clock

be proven false cannot be proven false
trust

settled now
falling down

so much moving
cobalt paint

maze-like
sugar alone

two-colored
thoughts crash

little one
out of bed

idle talk
reshape edge

shepherd's core
piping hot stones

at home
tattered & worn

unwrap me
but not too slow

## daily reminder

no reason for me to be experiencing these emotions
no reason for me to be feeling as anxious as i do as
　　often as i do
no reason for me to be destroying my relationships
　　with others so relentlessly

no reason for me to be

## one last haiku

we all were formed from
dead suns & there is something
beautiful in that.

# 7/7 (for kristie)

you're gone less than 2 months after i publish 2 of
your poems

i'm stocking groceries less than 15 minutes after i
hear that you're gone

i drop a box of bottles of olive oil & a slimy puddle
spreads

i stare at the oil spill & think about you being gone

you're gone but also not gone

you're not here anymore

you're wherever your grandmother is

you're with your grandmother that you loved &
mourned so much

before you were gone too

a coworker comes to the aisle & lifts the oil box

i hear glass shards shake inside the oil box like loose
bones

i hear "my immortal" by evanescence playing over the
store intercom

every cheesy muzak ballad suddenly sounds profound

grief makes us too emotional & sincere to care about
    being cheesy

this poem, for example, is cheesy

but sincerity was always your operative mode

before you were gone

less than 30 seconds after i write this poem, i'm
    putting cups of pudding on a shelf

and you're not here anymore

molly,

when kristie left last year, a poem left me easily~
a broken bottle of olive oil on a linoleum floor.
i didn't mean to because poems are worth so much
     less than
but the leak spread faster than i could sop at it. .

but your leaving & you~ i can only make out a trunk
with a hollowed-out hole the shape of a witch~
which is to say, an unknowable shape, not seen but
felt tingling all over, like after reading your words

or while eating a kookie or a kake of you or
your toasted coconut lamingtons,
the ones that should've won
on a season never aired.

i'm squinting at that shape in that bark through a fog
unable to see around to the other side of the wood,
but beside the tree i sense the sun of a hello'd halo~
hear a laugh like a chicken's cluck somewhere near &
     far.

~marzi

Marzi Margo is a person who writes & resides in Ohio. Ve is a very different person now than ve was when this book was first published several years ago. Ver most recent books are <u>yogaflowers</u> & <u>pink maggit</u>, both available from Ghost City Press. Ve tweets @wigglytuff_pink.

# More titles from Be About It Press

I've Been On Tumblr by Jesse Prado, 2014

Bye, Product by Catch Breath, 2015

Paper Flowers, Invisible Birds by Amy Saul-Zerby, 2017

I Love You, It Looks Like Rain by June Gehringer, 2018

Disaster Horse: Smol Essays by Nooks Krannie, 2019

A Pretty Little Wilderness by Cassandra Dallett, 2020

Be A Bough Tit by Richard Loranger, 2020

Double Rainbow by Lonely Christopher, 2021


Find out more on our website!
**beaboutitpress.com**

Follow **@baipress** on twitter